ESSENTIAL PRINCIPLES OF WRITING
Workbook

Essential Principles of Writing

© 2025 Dr. Chrishuna Harris-Griffin

All rights reserved. No part of this publication may be reproduced, distributed, or transmitted in any form or by any means, including photocopying, recording, or other electronic or mechanical methods, without the prior written permission of the publisher, except in the case of brief quotations used in critical reviews or certain other noncommercial uses permitted by copyright law.

Published by Morgan Hale Studios, LLC
Atlanta, Georgia
info@MorganHaleStudios.com

Author website: www.WritingWithDrChrissy.com
Illustrations by Morgan Hale

ISBN: 979-8-9940174-9-4
Printed in the United States of America
Second Edition, 2025

ESSENTIAL PRINCIPLES OF WRITING

Workbook

Table of Contents

Table of contents 4
Ethical Guidelines: Email Etiquette and Ethics................. 5
The Art of Professional Resignation 9
Ethical Guidelines in Professional Writing 17
The Essential Guideline of Essay Writing 22

Ethical Guidelines:

Email Etiquette and Ethics

Ethical Guidelines:
Email Etiquette and Ethics

Ethical email communication helps preserve professionalism, clarity, and trust in the workplace. By carefully considering subject lines, tone, and CC/BCC use, writers ensure their messages are both effective and respectful.

1. Subject Line

The subject line is the first impression your email makes and should accurately reflect the message's content and purpose. A clear, concise subject line helps recipients prioritize and respond appropriately. Misleading or vague subject lines (e.g., using "URGENT" unnecessarily) can damage your credibility and cause confusion. Ethical tip: Craft subject lines that are honest, respectful of the reader's time, and communicate your intent clearly.

2. Tone

Tone refers to the emotional quality or attitude conveyed in your writing. In professional settings, your tone should be respectful, courteous, and appropriate to the context.

Too casual? It may come off as unprofessional.

Too harsh or critical? It can escalate conflict or alienate the reader.

Ethical tip: Be mindful of tone, especially in emotionally charged situations.

3. CC and BCC Misuse

CC (Carbon Copy): Used to send a copy of an email to recipients in addition to the primary recipient. BCC (Blind Carbon Copy): Sends a copy of the email privately to others. BCC recipients are invisible to other recipients.

Common Misuses:

- Overusing CC can clutter inboxes and overwhelm recipients with irrelevant information.
- Misusing BCC may create distrust or violate confidentiality.

Ethical tip: Only include recipients who need the information. Be transparent about who is being copied. Never use CC/BCC to shame, surprise, or manipulate others.

CHECK FOR UNDERSTANDING

Ethical Guidelines: Email Etiquette and Ethics

Instructions: Use this worksheet to actively reflect on your current email practices and identify ways to align more closely with ethical communication standards. Read each section, then complete the prompts to apply what you've learned.

Subject Line

Read: The subject line sets the tone and expectation for your email. It should be clear, truthful, and respectful of your reader's time. Avoid vague or misleading phrases like "URGENT" if it isn't truly urgent.

Reflect & Apply:

- Write a subject line you recently used that may have been unclear or misleading:
  _____

- Rewrite it using clearer, more ethical language:
  _____

- What principles will guide how you write future subject lines?
  _____

Tone

Read: Tone reflects your attitude. Ethical writers aim for a respectful and courteous tone, even when dealing with conflict.

Reflect & Apply:

- Think of an email you sent where the tone could have been better: What was the situation?
  _____

- Rewrite one sentence from that email with a more ethical, collaborative tone: Original: _____ → Revised: _____

- Write a short prayer or intention to keep your communication grace-filled:
  _____
  _____

7

CC/BCC Use

Read: Use CC to keep relevant parties informed and BCC to protect privacy when necessary. Overuse or misuse of either can lead to ethical concerns.

Reflect & Apply:

- Have you ever CC'd someone unnecessarily or used BCC in a way that could be considered sneaky? Briefly describe the situation:
  _____

- How can you improve your decision-making around who to CC or BCC?
  _____

- Make a personal checklist for using CC and BCC ethically:

| ☐ Is this person directly involved? | ☐ Will this cause confusion or breach trust? | ☐ Am I using this to inform or to manipulate? |

Wrap-Up: Ethical Email Commitment

> **Write your personal commitment to practicing ethical email habits from today forward:**

☐ Your personal commitment
_____
_____
_____
_____
_____

Every email you send is a reflection of your character. Choose clarity, lead with respect, and let your communication reflect the excellence you bring to every space you enter.

The Art of Professional Resignation

A Complete Guide for Students

Understanding the Purpose and Importance of Resignation Letters

A resignation letter serves as the formal documentation of your decision to leave a position. For students entering the professional world, understanding this formality is crucial for career development. This written notice creates an official record of your departure date, helps your employer plan for your replacement, and sets the tone for how you'll be remembered after you leave.

Even in casual work environments or part-time student jobs, a well-crafted resignation letter demonstrates your professionalism and respect for workplace protocols. This document becomes part of your employment record and may be referenced when future employers contact your previous workplace for references.

Beyond its administrative function, a thoughtful resignation letter helps preserve the professional relationships you've built. The connections you make in early positions—even temporary ones during your academic career—can become valuable networking resources as you progress professionally. A proper resignation helps ensure these connections remain positive.

Creates an Official Record

Provides documentation of your departure date and intent to leave, protecting both you and your employer from misunderstandings.

Demonstrates Professionalism

Shows maturity and respect for workplace protocols, reflecting positively on your character and work ethic.

Preserves Relationships

Helps maintain positive connections with colleagues and supervisors who may become valuable references or networking contacts.

Facilitates Transition

Gives your employer time to prepare for your departure and arrange for the transfer of your responsibilities.

Regardless of your reason for leaving—whether it's to focus on studies, pursue another opportunity, or address personal circumstances—a properly formatted resignation letter shows that you understand professional expectations. This awareness of workplace etiquette is particularly valuable for students who are building their professional reputations and may need strong references for future opportunities.

Key Components and Proper Formatting

A well-structured resignation letter follows a standard business letter format. Each component serves a specific purpose in communicating your departure professionally. For students who may have limited experience with formal business correspondence, mastering this format is an excellent professional skill.

Header Information
Include your complete contact details (name, address, email, phone), the date, and your supervisor's information (name, title, company address).

Formal Salutation
Begin with "Dear [Manager's Name]," using their preferred title (Mr., Ms., Dr., etc.) and last name.

Resignation Statement
Clearly state your intention to resign, specify your position, and indicate your last working day (typically two weeks from submission date).

Transition Offer
Express willingness to assist with the transition process through training, documentation, or knowledge transfer.

Gratitude Expression
Thank your employer for the opportunities, mentioning specific skills or experiences gained that will benefit your academic or career path.

Professional Closing
End with "Sincerely," followed by your handwritten signature and typed name underneath.

Best Practices and Common Pitfalls

Writing an effective resignation letter requires balancing professionalism with sincerity. For students who may be leaving their first jobs, understanding these best practices will help create a positive lasting impression and avoid common mistakes that could damage relationships.

Essential Do's

- Keep your letter concise and focused—one page is typically sufficient
- Maintain a positive, professional tone throughout, even if you're leaving due to challenges
- Proofread carefully to eliminate spelling and grammatical errors
- Specify exactly when your last day will be
- Express genuine gratitude for the experience and opportunities
- Offer specific assistance for the transition period
- Mention skills or experiences gained that relate to your academic or career goals
- Submit your letter with adequate notice, respecting workplace policies

Critical Don'ts

- Include negative comments about colleagues, supervisors, or the organization
- Use emotionally charged language that reflects frustration or anger
- Share overly personal details about why you're leaving
- Brag about a better opportunity or higher salary elsewhere
- Make demands about final paychecks or benefits (address these separately)
- Submit without proofreading—errors reflect poorly on your attention to detail
- Use humor or casual language inappropriate for formal documentation
- Write an excessively long or overly detailed explanation of your departure

⊗ Emotional Writing Warning

If you're leaving due to negative circumstances (conflicts, dissatisfaction, etc.), draft your letter and wait 24 hours before reviewing it. This cooling-off period helps ensure you don't include impulsive statements that could damage your professional reputation. Remember that this document may be referenced years later when you're seeking full-time employment after graduation.

Emotional Writing Activity: Do's & Don'ts

For each statement, determine whether it represents a recommended action ("DO") or an action to avoid ("DON'T"). Write your answer in the blank provided.

Statement 1 (Example)
Thank your employer for the skills you've developed during your time there. DO

Statement 2 (Example)
Write two pages explaining every problem you encountered. DON'T

Statement 3
Offer to help train your replacement before leaving. ____

Statement 4
Tell your boss that your new job pays twice as much. ____

Statement 5
Proofread your letter for grammar and spelling mistakes. ____

Statement 6
Make jokes or use slang like you're texting a friend. ____

Statement 7
State clearly when your last day will be. ____

Statement 8
Include details about personal family conflicts. ____

DO's and DON'Ts Activity key - 3: DO, 4: DON'T, 5: DO, 6: DON'T, 7: DO, 8: DON'T

Sample Resignation Letters for Students

1

Standard Two-Week Notice Template

[Your Name]
[Your Address]
[City, State ZIP]
[Your Email]

[Date]

[Supervisor's Name]
[Their Title]
[Company Name]
[Company Address]
[City, State ZIP]

Dear [Supervisor's Name],

I am writing to formally resign from my position as [Your Position] at [Company Name], effective [Date – two weeks from submission].

I have valued the experience and skills I've gained during my time here, particularly [mention 1-2 specific skills or experiences]. These will benefit me as I [focus on my degree/transition to my next opportunity].

I am committed to ensuring a smooth transition during my remaining time. I would be happy to help train a replacement or document my current responsibilities.

Thank you for the opportunity to work with such a dedicated team.

Sincerely,

[Your Signature]
[Your Typed Name]

Sample Resignation Letters for Students

1

Academic Schedule Accommodation Sample

[Your Name]
[Your Address]
[City, State ZIP]
[Your Email]

[Date]
[Supervisor's Name]
[Their Title]
[Company Name]
[Company Address]
[City, State ZIP]

Dear [Supervisor's Name],

I am writing to formally resign from my position as [Your Position] at [Company Name]. My last day will be [Date – two weeks from submission].

As I enter a more demanding phase of my academic program, I need to dedicate more time to my studies. My upcoming course load requires additional focus, and I want to ensure I maintain the academic standards I've set for myself.

I am grateful for the flexibility [Company Name] has shown in accommodating my class schedule over the past [time period]. I am committed to helping with transition before my departure. I would be happy to assist in training my replacement if necessary.

Thank you for understanding my need to prioritize my education at this time. I have truly enjoyed working with the team!

Sincerely,

[Your Signature]
[Your Typed Name]

After Submission: Managing the Transition Period

1 — Day of Submission

Meet with your supervisor to discuss your resignation letter in person if possible. Be prepared to answer questions about your decision respectfully. Request any necessary information about final paycheck processing or returning company property.

2 — First Few Days

Begin documenting your processes and current projects. Create detailed instructions for recurring tasks. Make a list of ongoing responsibilities and their status. Inform key colleagues of your departure professionally without oversharing details.

3 — Middle of Notice Period

Train replacement if applicable. Transfer knowledge through shadowing sessions or documentation reviews. Update shared files and organize digital assets. Complete high-priority tasks that would be difficult for others to finish.

4 — Final Days

Return any company property (keys, ID badges, equipment). Send a professional farewell email to colleagues. Collect contact information from valued connections for networking. Complete exit interviews constructively if requested.

5 — After Departure

Send a thank-you note to your supervisor and key mentors. Update your resume and LinkedIn profile with skills gained. Maintain connections through appropriate professional networking. Respond promptly if contacted with transition questions.

Ethical Guidelines in Professional Writing

Honesty • Clarity • Confidentiality • Discretion

Honesty

Honesty in professional writing means ensuring that your communication is truthful, accurate, and transparent. Whether you're drafting an email, report, or recommendation:

 Do:

- Present factual information
- Credit original sources
- Include all relevant details

 Don't:

- Exaggerate or manipulate information
- Copy others' work without citation (plagiarism)
- Omit key facts that could distort understanding

Why it matters: Honesty builds your credibility and cultivates trust with readers. It ensures your message is received with integrity, reduces misunderstandings, and supports ethical decision-making within your organization.

Clarity

Clarity ensures that your message is easy to read, interpret, and respond to. Professional writing should use:

Do:

- Straightforward sentence structure
- Simple and direct language
- Correct grammar and punctuation

Don't:

- Use excessive jargon
- Be vague or wordy
- Intentionally obscure meaning to sound more "expert"

Why it matters: Clear writing respects the reader's time and promotes effective communication.

☐ Can you think of time when an unclear message caused chaos or confusion? Write about it below:

_____
_____
_____
_____

Confidentiality

Confidentiality refers to the ethical handling of sensitive or private information, including:

Employee records
Personnel files containing private information about employees that must be protected.

Internal business documents
Strategic plans, meeting minutes, and other sensitive corporate materials.

Financial or medical data
Highly regulated information that requires strict privacy controls.

Ethical writers:

- Only share information with authorized individuals
- Store documents securely
- Follow legal and organizational privacy guidelines

Why it matters: Violating confidentiality can break trust, damage reputations, and even lead to legal consequences.

Discretion

Discretion involves using good judgment when sharing information in a professional setting. It includes:

Do:
- Use a respectful tone
- Keep personal opinions appropriate and professional
- Understand your audience before sharing details

Don't:
- Gossip or speak negatively about others
- Overshare personal or sensitive opinions
- Use language that could be considered offensive or harmful

The Essential Guide to Middle School Essay Writing

Comprehensive Guide to Writing Outstanding Essays

Understanding Essay Structure

Introduction

Grabs the reader's attention with a hook and presents your thesis statement. This paragraph introduces your topic and gives readers a preview of what's to come.

Body

Contains multiple paragraphs that support your main idea. Each paragraph should focus on one specific point and include evidence or examples that back up your thesis.

Conclusion

Wraps up your essay by restating your thesis in different words and summarizing your main points. Leave readers with a final thought that makes your essay memorable.

Think of your essay like a sandwich: the introduction and conclusion are the bread that hold everything together, while the body paragraphs are the filling that provides substance. Each part has a specific purpose and works together to create a complete, satisfying whole.

Crafting a Strong Thesis Statement

The thesis statement is the heart of your essay—it's the main idea that controls everything you write. A strong thesis statement:

- Makes a specific claim or point about your topic
- Is typically just one sentence, located at the end of your introduction
- Tells readers exactly what to expect from your essay
- Keeps your writing focused and prevents you from going off-topic

> "A good thesis statement is clear, specific, and arguable—like a roadmap that guides both the writer and reader through the essay."

Exploring Different Essay Types

 ### Narrative Essay

Tells a story with characters, conflict, and sensory details. Often written in first person, these essays share personal experiences or fictional tales with a clear beginning, middle, and end.

 ### Expository Essay

Explains or informs about a topic using facts and examples. These essays are objective and straightforward, teaching readers about processes, comparisons, or cause-and-effect relationships.

 ### Persuasive Essay

Tries to convince the reader to agree with your opinion using logical arguments, emotional appeals, and credible evidence. These essays take a clear position on a debatable topic.

 ### Descriptive Essay

Paints a vivid picture using sensory details (sight, sound, smell, taste, touch). These essays bring scenes or objects to life through colorful language that appeals to the reader's imagination.

Understanding which type of essay you're writing helps you determine the appropriate tone, structure, and content. Each type serves a different purpose and requires specific writing techniques to be effective.

Common Transition Words

To add information: also, additionally, furthermore, moreover

To show cause/effect: therefore, consequently, as a result

To contrast: however, nevertheless, on the other hand

To sequence: first, next, then, finally, meanwhile

Revising and Editing Your Work

Revising (Big Picture)

Revising focuses on improving the overall content and organization of your essay. When revising, ask yourself these questions:

- Does my introduction grab attention and clearly state my thesis?
- Does each paragraph focus on one main idea with sufficient support?
- Do my ideas flow logically with smooth transitions?
- Does my conclusion effectively wrap up my main points?
- Have I included enough details and examples to support my points?

Peer Review

Ask a classmate, friend, or family member to read your essay and provide feedback. They might notice problems you missed or have suggestions for improvement.

Editing (Fine Details)

Editing focuses on correcting errors and improving clarity at the sentence level:

- Check for spelling errors (don't rely solely on spell-check)
- Correct grammar and punctuation mistakes
- Ensure consistent verb tense throughout
- Replace vague words with specific, vivid language
- Eliminate unnecessary repetition and wordiness

Try reading your essay aloud—this helps you catch errors your eyes might miss!

Reading Aloud

Hearing your words spoken helps identify awkward phrasing, run-on sentences, and areas where your writing doesn't flow smoothly.

Effective Prewriting Strategies

Why Prewriting Matters

Prewriting is like planning a road trip before you start driving. It helps you organize your thoughts, gather necessary information, and create a map for your writing journey. Taking time to plan will make the actual writing process much smoother and faster.

Studies show that students who spend time on prewriting activities typically produce better organized, more detailed essays than those who jump straight into drafting.

1 Brainstorming
Set a timer for 5 minutes and write down every idea related to your topic. Try mind mapping, listing, or freewriting to generate ideas.

2 Outlining
Create a roadmap for your essay with your thesis statement, main points of each paragraph, and supporting details organized in sequence.

3 Research & Note-taking
Gather facts, statistics, quotes, and examples that support your main points. Record sources carefully to create proper citations later.

Writing Strong Body Paragraphs

The body paragraphs are where you develop your ideas and provide evidence for your thesis. Each paragraph should focus on a single main idea and follow this structure:

Topic Sentence
Introduces the main idea of the paragraph and connects to your thesis

Supporting Details
Provides evidence, examples, facts, or explanations that develop the main idea

Analysis
Explains how your evidence supports your point and connects back to the thesis

Transition
Connects to the next paragraph with transition words or phrases